Bed is a powerful book of lucid and sensual poems. Metzger's lyric acuity reveals, in turn, the various ways in which the act of self-consciousness is both calm and disturbing. Her lines, in turn, and the spaces between them, enact what's so perilously poised in every instance of life, domestic or otherwise. She honours these moments with what one can only call incorrigible tenderness, of which, indeed, these poems are fiercely built, like an ark which has touched the bedrock of our human ardour. *Bed* is superb work.

ISHION HUTCHINSON
winner of the National Book Critics Circle Award

The wanting of a door, an exit made of the materiality and spirituality of a tree, Elizabeth Metzger's *Bed* investigates "the impermissible and the impermanent" where what can and cannot be recounted illustrates the terrors of intimacy and the ethereal knowing of empathy. Surface and reflection, doors and searchlights, embers and candles, God and theory, communion and nothingness, loss and desire, limbs and trunks and bodies, all call out from the simultaneity of time "searching for something other than silence," searching for "the infinite in real time." Metzger feeds her reader with stars from the beautiful tines of what I imagine as a silver George Jensen fork, for she is an "angel of wait" and though her poems dread the Kafkaesque night and not night, they turn that human terror of existence into a ethereal sense of meaning that uncannily soothes the soul. Her sculpted, sensuous powerful, crafted language is a tour de force poetic enactment of what it means to exist. Sit on the grass and look up at the sky, and then read this brilliant book now.

ELIZABETH A.I. POWELL
author of *Atomizer*

BE D

BE D

POEMS

ELIZABETH METZGER

TUPELO PRESS
2021

ISBN-13: 978-1-946482-60-0
Library of Congress LCCN: 2021936781

Cover and text design by adam b. bohannon.

First paperback edition November 2021.

Tupelo Press
P.O. Box 1767
North Adams, Massachusetts 01247
(413) 664-9611 / Fax: (413) 664-9711
editor@tupelopress.org / www.tupelopress.org

Tupelo Press is an award-winning independent literary press that publishes fine fiction, non-fiction, and poetry in books that are a joy to hold as well as read. Tupelo Press is a registered 501(c)(3) non-profit organization, and we rely on public support to carry out our mission of publishing extraordinary work that may be outside the realm of the large commercial publishers. Financial donations are welcome and are tax deductible.

Dread of night. Dread of not-night.

FRANZ KAFKA

CONTENTS

BE D

Won Exit

In one or two lives
I opened the door with the prize
only to find the prize was not worth the life.

I wanted the door.

Brave mahogany door, you be my fortune.
Teach me to understand the cry
in your grain, the suffering circles

by which your tree wisdom is known.

I was superior with handles,
gentle with thresholds. Then, this.

Choices at morning hours I usually skip
but there is a little cashflow of beauty
where there is almost no more water.

And there is not room and light enough
to stand behind the second
and listen anymore—

I am going through the language of me now.

I am flipping open the dictionary of myself
with my tongue, as if that were possible,
to find your first word.

In the torture of a foyer
doorless for entering, I am entering none.

With Wayward Motion

The wind parted me.
Wind from nowhere.

It did not get up
from its snoring carriage

or offer me a bottled
sense of the near future.

It did not cry
so much as moan

into the mouth of a
passing monument.

There goes my self
with invisible scissors

narrowing my loves,
dusting the pollen

off Spring like another
previous opportunity.

We argued about what
could be unconditional.

We forgot to pay.
We forgot to die

was also our only chance
to be infinitive

in real time. One of us
loved the other like

an instrument that
would not ever again

be played
though it was perfectly

strung and oiled.
Mother love came up

and of course children
but what about their

scrotums and egg sacs.
Could we already adore

those in extremis?
The wind was all over

my face reminding me
of my other affairs:

The impermissible.
The impermanent.

The sex between all
who already possessed

themselves and were
satisfied, not by me.

Sex Dream

What part of lying still
left room for missing you? I missed the floor,
I missed letting the shower hit my stomach
without consequence. Then
I missed the nurse.

I did not miss violence, not passion.
I still had those, if hidden.

Never longed for a moment to last.
Never thought of the night
your hand
brought out the wet proof of my own life.

I was for the first time neutral,
the only angel of wait,
all the weeks one page
I was graceful at turning. Will you ever open me
the old way and not be wrecked,
I did not expect to ever ask you.

Exaggerated Honey

Once there was nobody left to love
a family had me.

My mother made a steeple with her hands
that folded open to reveal no people.

Show me again, I said. Tell me again
not to talk to strangers.

The hospital lights across the street
taught me to stay awake in my own company.

Later I asked strangers to take my hand
across. I used to think I hated where I came from

and would leave, that children elsewhere
found safety in freedom, but there is no fire

anywhere I am capable of rubbing.
I am not mother enough to tolerate

creating my own heat, not human enough
to gather close to what's untouchable.

Call me complaint. Call me *honey you exaggerate*.
When my family laughs in the hallway

I laugh with my hair thrown back to the ground
like I understand them. Just to be answered,

I take it as seriously as the dead
or a bridge to nowhere. But what loss on earth

would I honestly like to stay for? And life
is no better, thank god. It also keeps us.

You've Been on Earth So Long Already

All my life all I've wanted was to be myself
and someone else. Not theirs but them.

My shame about this greed made
me hesitant with other children.

I wanted what they wanted, but apart:

I tried to make it, spooned what I could
in shallow mental dishes I stacked
all night and poured through

my neediest hole, which opens only
for medicine or extreme misunderstanding.

My teeth browned from too much
thirst too late.

My eyes bulged from noticing
what I wasn't meant to be.

There was a playground which I went to
—and can't take you.

The first thing I did daily
was look for a place to hide, or flee.
There were plenty of gates and wide enough trees

but I stayed off-center, just beyond
the sprinkler's way.

The other children played until they snacked
around me. Sometimes they cried.
Sometimes they looked consoled by what they couldn't have.

No not now
The boundary of things. The boundary of time.
I wish this for you—come soon—to be withheld.

They were so freely asking for more world.

First Wound Kept Open

The thought
of all the grass

blown over to one side
hurts me. That wind

can do that. I must have
gotten to him first

though he pushed out against
the little pouch in me

I now call soulless.
Of everyone I've met

on earth I always find
they got here first

and will they teach
me their good

reason for staying?
I would discipline

a comet against
my way of leaving,

push it out of sky after
sky and after

every loss on earth
the baby I was

would come back. That's
what it means to be lovable,

to give oneself whole
again whole birth

whole placenta whole
breast whole milk

whole fist whole flower
but only what fits

harmlessly whole
in the mouth.

The baby comes and goes,
comes back to weed me

of my body, feeds my
bald birdies

what's not for me to know.
I had hoped that all

my animosity toward men
would lead toward

safety in one who
would wake me before

I hit the wooden world
and rock me there

to say what violence
had not yet come.

Moses, New York

There was a boat on the pond
but no water. The water had sacrificed

itself for your brutal thirst. Goodbye,
cowboys. Goodbye, not knowing

to speak.

The boat is ready for me, baby.
Enough with the reeds and the motherless.

One singular horn
will turn your face purple.

A leaf blower may take your breath away.

But the boat here is always
and human. It floats on nothing.

All the surfaces for floating
and reflecting are gone. What good is

what passes through us but clouds?

There is a branch overhead
as if there were birds. And I would rather

show you than go.

The God Incentive

He kept me through childhood.
There was a reason
he kept me from sin like a biscuit
warming in the oven.

It's okay I tell the rain to keep him a theory
but bring him down
once in a while.

It's okay to be honest or selfish
but find the spot where you sink
a little into the velvet stadium seat
of secrets other secrets
have rubbed away.

See I have been alone and didn't know it
waiting on the inside glass
of a trafficked world
where one mistrust passes another
with a long yellow horn
that no hand can quiet.

Something other than science
is pressing down on my night watch
saying sing here
instead of signing off this hour.

Ride the hard part,
that is the good part as many holy animals
must know and let go of,
everyone is still barely alive.

The Witching Hour

In life
if I could say for sure

what I have loved
there would be

no tunnel needed
for any inner

or earthly transport.
Everywhere

I turned
there would appear

only the blinding clubs
of the sun

and when I thought
of escape

I would thank
a dead man

for my thoughts
and lick

through his navel
all my sweet unknowable

time. He would be lanky
and love and

unlove me.
I would not worry

about our undoing,
about survivals.

I would get up from bed
and be gone

with the kit of the careless.
In my confusion

I would have a child.
I already did. I did

him a fatal injury
bringing him here.

They handed him
out of my body

onto my body.
When he cried I misled him

with joy, beckoned
by something that knew

my hands better than I,
toward the soft spot

of earth. It was not
childhood. I'm a mother now

and I can promise
under the grown breast

the heart is still changeable
that far down.

When I grieve
he plays with the salt.

He hangs on the
faulty edge

of my face. I have him uneven.
I have him to hold

my life open
like a towel

and take my pains
then feed me one star

on a fork and say
no big deal.

Mercy Later

There is this green chair to which I don't belong.
I keep it in the middle of every room I enter
including yours.

Threading repetitive leaves remind me
I never traveled far for anyone but myself.
Hi, hi you say to the green, the turned-away talkers.

I ran today with you sort of in my arms
toward the ambulances, full of joy and appetite
for emergency   *we oh we oh*

we thought we were giddy in the siren sunlight.
It turns out a woman just died crossing here.
And then we walked the second half of the blockaded street,

you hushing and roaring more
with each approaching pair of police motorcycles
on either side of the buckling road.

Everyone including you earned half my hate.
I can't say if I ever enjoyed anything
except coming home

                    to the green chair
I keep in the middle of my room
and how sorry I feel that I can't wheel you

out of one state into another,
how you'll never know me alone with a word,
and I won't see you flinch your eyes open

to a planet other than earth or a body on earth
you have floored, or carry you high,
deposit you on the top of the slide

like it's safe,
sorry for a bird I once used in a poem
whom I never thought again of,

how I can't forget where and what
you're driving in me
even though you no longer belong here.

The Impossibility of Crows

Your death has just begun but it is not
spoken of, it speaks
in odd weathers like a second first love

as if the snow could fall for real here
as if you would deign to visit me through sun.

There are no directions

the edges of your death are smudged and round
like ash or a watch
whose accuracy is the least of its beauty.

There is no clear ill will
there is no bronzy heaven.

You will come to me instead
though I never came to you
won't you?

It's not too late yet
it isn't blood or sex
it isn't even the spirit or
splinted ambition.

Today I will stay for
just the last unafraid adoring avalanche of you

as if my life had wound itself up
and let go with yours

a made metal crow
acting born

choosing its cracktime
then tiptoeing off your branch of the world.

Early Rising

When the earth took away my fires
I sighed in bodies

I mean the sighs had limbs and trunks
and as with bodies

some were living
some not
some almost
or almost headless

like the ember I thought was over
before it blew up into a planet

mostly water and everything connected was a kinder island

it did not betray the aims of water

it did not bury what my hands have buried
or nurture
what your hands have warmed
then scorched

before I took
away my earth

my earths were buried

and I rubbed apart their pieces
for your fire

put me out
put me where I don't forgive by heart

Marriage

You want to know what I actually love?
It is the mind I don't have access to
Like a flower cut and placed on a kitchen table,
Looking more like a human body than
It could in the field with its kind. What does species matter,
Things die please remind me
When I say I don't feel anything, and then
It is better for them to be broken down
Again, a powder once fertile
And original. Now
In need of none of those powers.
Let me try saying it again, I don't feel anything
So something can die
Further down, yes like that
Like the last time I came across
A flower that wasn't planted. We don't have to
Make it actual, no more wild purpose of hands.

Rolling Out

Our desire diminished like oxen,
discarded us.

I watched them roll at first oblivious
into my embarrassment

playfully then responsibly then
like motes of hurricane light

they amassed their almost absentee
hides into one

                viable smallness.

And while small
it was enough to be acknowledged
as something to see by

so lit up were they in their burning to be seen.

I pretended your true feeling was hidden
in mine

                between other animal sounds
                repeating,

maybe submitted with horns
to the blind hill and dust

of the multiplying child we roam.
Night, no.

There is no guardian
for the one we never got.

                    Then our desire
started doing the things it thought we liked.

One More Day

After people I kept rolling away rocks

to let the plumes pass—why
was I here again

testing the depth of the smoke
with the back of my hand.

Things had been going hellishly for a long while
which meant many were making me hate

and now just me—

a voice I couldn't place called out
saying maybe the fire will save the house,

did it mean spare.

There had been another flare up
and I welcomed the staticky cry.

It did not ask for my help and I did not offer.

I was still counting down days to a new conception
instead of

hosing down the straw houses of my neighbors.

Ash landed on my cheek
it was a ladybug—

I didn't even know what it was until it flew off in a gust.

There is a lot about others I don't remember,
outliving an interest.

What is the point, the same voice said,

of remembering you are not the only one
blowing yourself down.

Godface

Once I sat straining to keep you whole
when Max said

look up
that high window was made to keep you aware
of an exit you can't access
but will be forced through.
You will want the exact pain then
you would die of now.

         He said
look down
the mosaic tiles are not just a cold
assembly of random glass.
They are what god is, individual for each
of us, a face designed
with all our dead
in novel arrangements—
friends, ancestors, strangers,
even what has not yet lived.

So you are here, and there still
making up my godface,
and if by winter you raise your eyes
into this dimension,

you will already have renamed the places
where my body touches
through this one-room world.

Almost One

I have no twins left.
The reflection of my room in the window is so convincing

it goes on,
the placement of furniture identical
& appreciated & I'm not visible looking out.

To surpass the reflection.
To hunt the suburban night
for wheels on your behalf.

There is another mind here—

It will start to ask me how things work.
I dread it.

Doors don't just open & close,
people leave them open people leave them closed.

When you ask me one night far away
like a searchlight across the underworld
would I come get you, give you life all over,
I say   *I would.*

                    I say it easily because this night
the arts have stopped &
if there are recurring voices

demanding my presence, expecting another birth
they do only the harm of
crickets, only the good.

Last of Kin

We came with others where
we came alone.

Though it was world we never saw it whole.

There were seasons. There were senses.

Time called to space but the phone was
off the hook, old phone.

In a dark home an instant more by choice,
the body.

What else was instantaneous

the air
how we destroyed it.

God, or our last child
made to make ourselves believe in…
an excuse from language

what we couldn't know,
how paper tears most completely once torn a little.

We were moving when we thought we were most still.

We had nowhere else to go.

Say Nothing

I go home to my dead
try to want less

the communion with my closest candle

—not worry about the color
the stick part the wax staining the wood

or the table standing through
the do-you-feel-it earthquake.

What are the chances I'll be struck by that.

Forget the fire I have done fire.
I haven't burned anything without planning.

There is a man that stays away in me
as if he already missed my daylife.

He never found words and is either too old
or too young.

Try to go back to shy smiles
slow appetite

a dress that floats up on a bus

through the daydreams of strangers.
With a lantern—that kind of child.

Was it mine, my daydream

awareness, even then it was the awareness
that made me more despicable.

Some were wrongful I'm sure

they did want more than
to pinch my cheeks and

rode the elevator just to find me

and some were caretakers as they claimed,
if only I had let them adore me.

Desire

It is for you I put the children to bed.

Or, come. I will keep the house awake for you.

The floor is fluttering with tongues.
I step through and you step after me
                                              laughing,
these are toys.

                    Isn't it obvious how we've changed?

I have no more use for pure feeling.
You escape directly behind my head.

Little vitrines in the closed museums
not being looked at
                    I would die to be their objects.

The children left me.
You say they came.

What could you possibly do for my body
when I am in two

                    separate rooms,
                    breathing?

On a Clear Night

I have broken our heart again. I have made the animal
noise the animal, you know I make up
what I don't know. I used to think that was resilience.

If I could speak with an earlier you
I would say have I told you what will happen to us,
and you would laugh trusting I knew.

All I would have to do is read, really read in front of you.
Do you see my relationship to my face?
I wish to pull myself out of it. Of course I can't

but I love wishing. No matter how much I tell you
there is as much I cannot tell you.

ACKNOWLEDGMENTS

Thank you to the editors of the following journals and websites in which the poems in *Bed* first appeared (sometimes in earlier versions):

The Academy of American Poets' *Poem-a-Day*, *American Poetry Review*, *The Common*, *The Laurel Review*, *Narrative Magazine*, *The Nation*, *The New Yorker*, *The Paris Review*, *Poetry Magazine*, *Poetry Northwest*, *The Yale Review*.

Bed's epigraph comes from Franz Kafka's *Blue Octavo Notebooks* by way of Lucie Brock-Broido. The title "The Impossibility of Crows" is a phrase I borrowed from Kafka's *The Zurau Aphorisms*.

The poems in *Bed* were written before, during, between, and after two bedridden pregnancies, for my children and in memory of the poets Max Ritvo and Lucie Brock-Broido, two great spirits who continually bring me back to life even from their afterlife. My best company during bed rest.

Thank you to Lisa Park for giving me dignity at my sickest and for caring for me with love and skill. To Estelle Shane for keeping me sane enough to find poetry no matter what. To the doctors, nurses, and champions whose care allowed and inspired my words and changed the direction of my life.

To Timothy Donnelly, Dorothea Lasky, Lia Kohl, Sylvia Linsteadt, and Elsinore Smidth-Carabetta, whose visions inspired me while writing *Bed*. To Jean Valentine whose voice feels close to my ear even as I miss her earthly correspondence terribly. To the many friends, teachers, readers, and artists whose eyes passed through these pages and whose words and love passed through my brain— thank you for supporting me during transformation, joy, and despair. I am a poet because you make me a person.

Thank you especially to the judge, Mark Bibbins, for selecting *Bed* as the winner of the Sunken Garden Poetry Prize. To everyone at Tupelo Press, especially Jeffrey Levine and Kristina Marie Darling, and David Rossitter, who made *Bed* a real dream in chapbook form. Thank you for believing in my work. To adam bohannon, who designed a cover to hold these poems, and Yvette Roman, who made me feel like a poem. To Elizabeth A.I. Powell and Ishion Hutchinson for their generous gift of words.

To the readers I haven't met, you give *Bed* ongoing life.

To my family, above all to Dan, first reader and first love, who helped bring these poems to life. Thank you for our life.

To my children, again and always, for existing and for offering me perpetual awe. Many of these poems come from my wish for your existence, and the shock of it. With and without language I love you and wish for you everything.

ABOUT THE AUTHOR

Yvette Roman

Elizabeth Metzger is the author of *The Spirit Papers*, winner of the Juniper Prize for Poetry, and the chapbook *The Nutshell Studies of Unexplained Death*. Her poems have appeared in *The New Yorker*, *The Paris Review*, *Poetry Magazine*, *American Poetry Review*, *The Nation*, and the Academy of American Poets' *Poem-a-Day*. Her prose has appeared in *Conjunctions*, *Literary Hub*, *Guernica*, and *Boston Review*. She is a poetry editor at *The Los Angeles Review of Books*. She can be found at elizabethmetzger.com

SUNKEN GARDEN POETRY AT HILL-STEAD MUSEUM

Sunken Garden Poetry began almost thirty years ago in Farmington, Connecticut, with a single poetry reading in the magical setting of Hill-Stead Museum's Sunken Garden, drawing huge crowds even that first year. Since then the annual series has become one of the premiere and best-loved venues for poetry in the country, featuring the top tier of American poets as well as emerging and student writers from the region. From its inception this poetry festival has given equal weight to the quality of text and the poet's ability to deliver an engaging, powerful, and entertaining experience in the unique theater of the Sunken Garden.

Out of the festival have grown competitions, year-round workshops and events, and an educational outreach to Hartford high schools. And while centered at Hill-Stead—with its beautiful views, Colonial Revival house, and priceless collection of Impressionist paintings—Sunken Garden Poetry now engages an ever-wider audience through a growing online presence; an online poetry journal, *Theodate*; public radio broadcasts; and an annual chapbook prize, co-published by Tupelo Press.

SUNKEN GARDEN CHAPBOOK POETRY PRIZE

2021

Bed by Elizabeth Metzger

SELECTED BY MARK BIBBINS

Let me confess to having taken the easy way in. My mind first went to the noun (where we sleep), then to the verb ("to sleep with"). Yours may have too, but the more time you spend with this remarkable book, the more you might come to think of planting, tending, picking. A bed of roses—or indeed, no bed of roses. Elizabeth Metzger's poems act as both repositories and engines of mystery, of "secrets other secrets / have rubbed away," yet their mysteriousness never feels coy. There's a difference between hiding information and asserting control over how it's revealed. "I stayed off-center," she writes, and to me this has always seemed like one of the better places from which to view things, but hers is furthermore a poetry that recognizes, as Gertrude Stein put it, "there is no use in a center." Among Metzger's many gifts is her ability to describe complicated positions simply, facing down the conundrums of language and perspective to devastating effect: "The children left me. / You say they came."

—from the Judge's Citation by Mark Bibbins

2020

Salat by Dujie Tahat

SELECTED BY CORNELIUS EADY

2019

Diurne by Kristin George Bagdanov

SELECTED BY TIMOTHY DONNELLY

2018

Flight by Chaun Ballard

SELECTED BY MAJOR JACKSON

2017

Ordinary Misfortunes by Emily Jungmin Yoon

SELECTED BY MAGGIE SMITH

2016

Feed by Suzanne Parker

SELECTED BY JEFFREY LEVINE AND CASSANDRA CLEGHORN

2015

Fountain and Furnace by Hadara Bar-Nadav

SELECTED BY PETER STITT

2014

We Practice For It by Ted Lardner

SELECTED BY MARK DOTY